KU-428-971

A Picture of a
Moment in Time

Rob Birkbeck

The Dudley Metropolitan Borough
at the Dawn of the New Millennium
1999-2000

Above: *The Waterfront complex, Brierley Hill, irradiates light across the still waters of the adjacent canal boat basin.* **Previous page:** *Dudley Castle by night.*

A Picture of a Moment in Time

Rob Birkbeck

The Dudley Metropolitan Borough
at the Dawn of the New Millennium
1999-2000

International
Projects
and
Publications

4197

Copy number of
6,500 copies

A Picture of a Moment in Time
The Dudley Metropolitan Borough
at the Dawn of the New Millennium

© Rob Birkbeck, 1999

Published by International Projects & Publications
P.O. Box 1609, Stourbridge, West Midlands
DY8 1ZE, United Kingdom

intlprojects@cwcom.net
www.dudley2000.mcmail.com

All photographs, other than those acknowledged on page 167,
  © 1999 by Rob Birkbeck

Illustrated Cartography on pages 14 & 15, © 1999 by Dudley Marketing Initiative,
  used with permission

Design and photo editor, Vanessa Birkbeck
Final layout, Michelle Yap Siew Keow, Colourscan, Singapore
Text abridgement, Rob Birkbeck

Origination by Colourscan Co. Pte. Ltd., Singapore
Printing & binding by Star Standard Industries Co. Pte. Ltd., Singapore

A single printing of 6,500 individually numbered copies

Special Edition (500 copies), cloth bound, ISBN 0 9536488 0 X
Celebration Edition (6,000 copies) ISBN 0 9536488 1 8

A CIP catalogue for this book is available from the British Library

All rights reserved. No part of this publication may be reproduced, stored in a retrieval
system, or transmitted, in any form or by any means, electronic, mechanical, photo-
copying, recording or otherwise, without the permission of the publisher or author.

Mary Stevens Park, Stourbridge.

Special Thanks

Thanks are due to Jane Surman of the Dudley Marketing Initiative who kindly opened many doors for me and who has been a constant source of encouragement and support at all times. Her insight into the Borough has greatly assisted my work.

With sincere and grateful thanks to those who have helped in the compilation of this work particularly those who have written one of the section forewords or helped me with the captions;

John Billingham, Kevin Clements, Adrian Durkin, Nick Fazey, John Fergusson, Steve Field, Lynn Foord, Trevor Genge, Charles Hajdamach, John Hemmingway, Jack Haden, Jill Hitchman, Tony Hitchmough, Stan Hill, David Radmore, Tom Slater, Geoff Warburton, Ian Waldon & Andy Webb.

Thanks too to the ladies at the Dudley Tourist Centre whose wealth of knowledge has been a rich source of information and whose careful direction has helped guide my path and fuel my enthusiasm.

And to the many others who have stopped, for a moment, to show me the way, to reflect on the past, to smile for the camera and to help me record a glimpse of their lives and surroundings.

Apology

If for any reason I have omitted any particular historical feature, landmark, hamlet, street or activity it is not because I am biased or favour one thing or area over the other. All have their unique importance and character and all help to form the kaleidoscope of images that are the Dudley Borough. It is simply because of lack of space.

I have amassed over 2,500 photographs, most of them quite worthy of inclusion yet only some 10% could make it into this book. For me this was the hardest part, leaving out that hillside meeting, that gratefully received dawn cup of tea, that 'up to my knees in mud' experience, memories of the Borough that will live with me forever. Please forgive me. I trust however, that as each person that I have met on this journey has influenced my life, that in this book you will find a gallery of images that will evoke and rekindle memories of your own special place, your own treasured view or very own unique, moments in time.

The imposing south portico
of Himley Hall at night.

Contents

Dedication

I dedicate this book to my wife Vanessa and my precious children, Rachael, James, Danielle and Paul who have, over the years, watched Dad take on all sorts of projects necessitating, late hours and long journeys. May each one of you follow the God-given desires of your heart, pursuing only that which is upright, honest and noble.

The dawn of the new Millennium, a milestone in history.
The seven mile peg on the Wolverhampton to Stourbridge road.

Foreword

Rob Birkbeck

If our house were burning down, most of us would not rescue our televisions or computers, despite the many hours they consume. After the family itself, most of us would try to save the photos. For they, like the lives they record, are irreplaceable.

A photograph may be an enduring image, but the moment it freezes is so fleeting. We only celebrate the Millennium once, and then it is gone. But it is a milestone which can project our past into our future. For the hopes of tomorrow spring only from the lessons of yesterday.

And because we record history, we absorb those lessons from our forebears; iron men and women who laid the mighty stones of the Dudley Castle; whose lives mingled with the molten steel of the industrial revolution and who breathed the first steam from the mighty steam engines; who carved canal tunnels through the heart of the earth and who forged the Titanic's anchors and her crystal glasses. The lives of these individuals impacted the world and changed history and the memory of each are woven into the very fabric of our own experience. Cobb's engine at Bumble Hole reverberates no longer to the beat of the steam engine; the deep, dark caverns that once pulsed with the hammer of workmen lie quiet, save for the drip of water. Yet these shadows of a former glory each bear testimony to the resourcefulness, creativeness and sheer determination of those whose lives have gone before. The embers at the foot of the towering Wordsley glass cone have long gone cold, yet the fire in the hearts of those who worked to build the area in which we live, lives on.

Rob Birkbeck

Those in the Dudley Borough look to its past with pride yet look forward to their future with optimism and hope. The Borough's towns and hamlets are each a rich source of history yet all bear testimony of its forward looking future. It is a place of people, panoramas, nature and life … if we would only take a moment to stop and look.

'*A Picture of a Moment in Time*' seeks to showcase a little of the character of the Borough, to testify of her achievements, and celebrate her beauty. Let the images within, stir in you a sense of wonder at the place in which we live and the lives of those who have gone before. May they evoke in the minds of the more senior amongst us a kaleidoscope of memories and may they implant in the hearts of the young, a vision, a dream and a goal for the future.

R. Birkbeck.

Rob Birkbeck

The Council House, Dudley

The Mayor of Dudley

Councillor Fred Hunt

Being at the heart of the Black Country it is easy to see the Borough of Dudley as an historical artifact. The landscape harks back to the industrial revolution and to the coal and steel industries which gave the Black Country its name. The Castle bears witness to the powerful Earls of Dudley and the canals to the power of commerce to overcome the natural landscape.

I would hate it if people just thought of Dudley as some sort of industrial heritage park. Yes, our landscape still bears the scars of the mining and smelting that occupied previous generations. And yes, 'metal bashing' is still a significant part of the local economy. However, the Borough is of the modern day and not just because Dudley Metropolitan Borough was created in 1974 to include the former Municipal Boroughs of Halesowen and Stourbridge, but because the skills and ingenuity of the local people have triumphed again and again.

In place of steel works scattered throughout the Borough we now have one of the largest shopping complexes in Europe alongside a similarly large office development which is home to companies serving the whole of the UK. We now find ourselves on the threshold of the new Millennium, in a place our forebears would find familiar yet, on closer inspection, completely different. And that is as it should be.

The Millennium is merely a moment in time in which we choose to contemplate the past, present and future and to celebrate the achievements of Dudleans past and present. For Dudley the Millennium gives us the chance to emerge from our heritage, to reach out into the future and make our history anew.

This book is part of the celebration of what we have achieved. I am delighted that Rob has produced such an elegant postscript to Dudley's Millennium.

I would also like to take this opportunity to wish everyone the best for the new Millennium and to hope that this one will be remembered for peace, love and understanding.

His Worship the Mayor of Dudley,
Councillor Fred Hunt

His Worship the Mayor of Dudley,
Councillor Fred Hunt

The Dudley Metropolitan Borough. Faces from all walks of life.

The Dudley Metropolitan Borough

As its residents well know, the Borough of Dudley has always been a fascinating place to live and work – and is never more so than now, at the start of the third Millennium.

Spanning an area of nearly 38 square miles, situated on the western side of the West Midlands conurbation, the landscape is as diverse and varied as its character. Its young and old people, its towns, villages, countryside and industry, its green space, parks and buildings, all combine together to make it a unique place of surprising contrast.

Today's thriving Borough is built upon a rich industrial heritage, but the ease at which the landmarks of the past sit with the developments of the present and future is truly remarkable. The vast canal network, which once supported the commercial growth of the Borough is now navigated by those seeking a more leisurely experience; land that once played host to heavy industry is now home to vibrant high tech businesses; major investment by large national and international organisations who have chosen to base their work locally; all give testimony to Dudley's vibrant entrepreneurial spirit.

Apart from a busy commercial life which gives us one of the country's highest rates of employment, the Borough also boasts of wonderful buildings, from the grandeur of its stately homes to the quirky eccentricity of its cozy pubs. Its beautiful parklands including The Leasowes in Halesowen, laid out in the 18th century by the poet William Shenstone, one of the first natural landscaped gardens in Europe is now being rebuilt to reflect his original vision. Stunning open countryside and farmland is on our doorstep, and the Borough can be proud of its many parks, nature reserves and open places.

Today's beautiful landscape however, was once covered by shallow tropical seas full of coral reefs and 425 million years ago it was home to Dudley's oldest resident – the 'Dudley Bug'. In an area which is now world-famous for its fascinating marine fossils, this little trilobite holds great local significance … in the last century, quarrymen found them so frequently that it was even incorporated into Dudley's coat of arms. From its ancient geological wealth to the Borough's more recent treasure – its 400 year old glass trade. Some of the world's most recognisable brands (including Royal Doulton, Stuart Crystal and Royal Brierley to name just three) sit side-by-side with a new generation of exciting and innovative studio glass artists, combining a thriving industry with a major tourist attraction.

Dudleans are well known to work hard and play hard and few places can offer such a variety of leisure experiences in such close proximity. From the hilltop Dudley Zoo and Castle to the longest navigable canal tunnel in Britain, the living history of the Black Country Living Museum to the stylish Waterfront with its bars and restaurants.

The new Millennium will indeed be a time to take pride in the heritage upon which the Dudley Borough was built, to celebrate today's incredible diversity and dynamism and to look forward with optimism to the potential of our tomorrow.

The Dudley Metropolitan Borough

1. Dudley Castle

2. Dudley Zoo

3. Black Country Living Museum

4. Bonded Warehouse

5. Stuart Crystal & Glass Cone

6. Broadfield House Glass Museum

7. Royal Doulton
8. Royal Brierley Crystal
9. The Crystal Glass Centre
10. Staffordshire Crystal
11. Dennis Hall Tudor Crystal
12. Brierley Hill Glass Co

13. Himley Hall & Park

14. Priory Ruins
15. St. Mary's Abbey

16. Dudley Museum & Art Gallery

17. Wren's Nest National Nature Reserve

18. Lodge Farm Reservoir
19. Buckpool and Fens Pools Nature Reserve
20. Bumble Hole Nature Reserve

21. The Leasowes
22. Saltwells Local Nature Reserve including Doulton's Claypit
23. Mary Stevens Park
24. Kinver Edge
25. Baggeridge Country Park
26. Stevens Park

27. Cotwall End Countryside & Craft Centre
28. Hawbush Urban Farm

29. Merry Hill & The Waterfront
30. Dudley Market Place & Churchill Centre
31. The Ryemarket Centre & Crown Shopping Centre
32. The Cornbow Centre

33. Crooked House
34. Little Dry Dock
35. The Vine
36. The Fountain
37. The Park Inn
38. The Beacon Hotel
39. The Jolly Crispin
40. The Britannia (Sally's)
41. The Lamp Tavern
42. The Waggon & Horses
43. The Nailmaker
44. The Blue Brick
45. The Park Tavern
46. The Why Not
47. The Black Horse

48. Halfpenny Green Vineyards & Winery

49. Lye Balti Houses

50. Halesowen Leisure Centre
51. Crystal Leisure Centre
52. Dudley Leisure Centre
53. Brierley Hill Leisure Centre
54. Coseley Swimming Pool

55. Dell Stadium
56. Halesowen Athletic & Cycling Club

57. Himley Hall Golf Centre
58. Sedgley Golf Centre

59. Dudley Town Hall
60. Stourbridge Town Hall
61. Brierley Hill Civic Hall
62. Cornbow Hall

63. Netherton Arts Centre

64. Halfpenny Green Airport

65. Stourbridge College
66. Halesowen College
67. Dudley College
68. King Edward VI College, Stourbridge
69. Oldswinford Hospital School, Stourbridge
70. University of Wolverhampton, Dudley Campus

 Information Centre

●—— Railway Line

- - - 🚲 Cycle Route

B Main Bus Stations

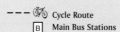

This map is intended for use as a guide only to the location of attractions and amenities in the Borough of Dudley.
It is suggested that it is used in conjunction with a detailed road map or A-Z.

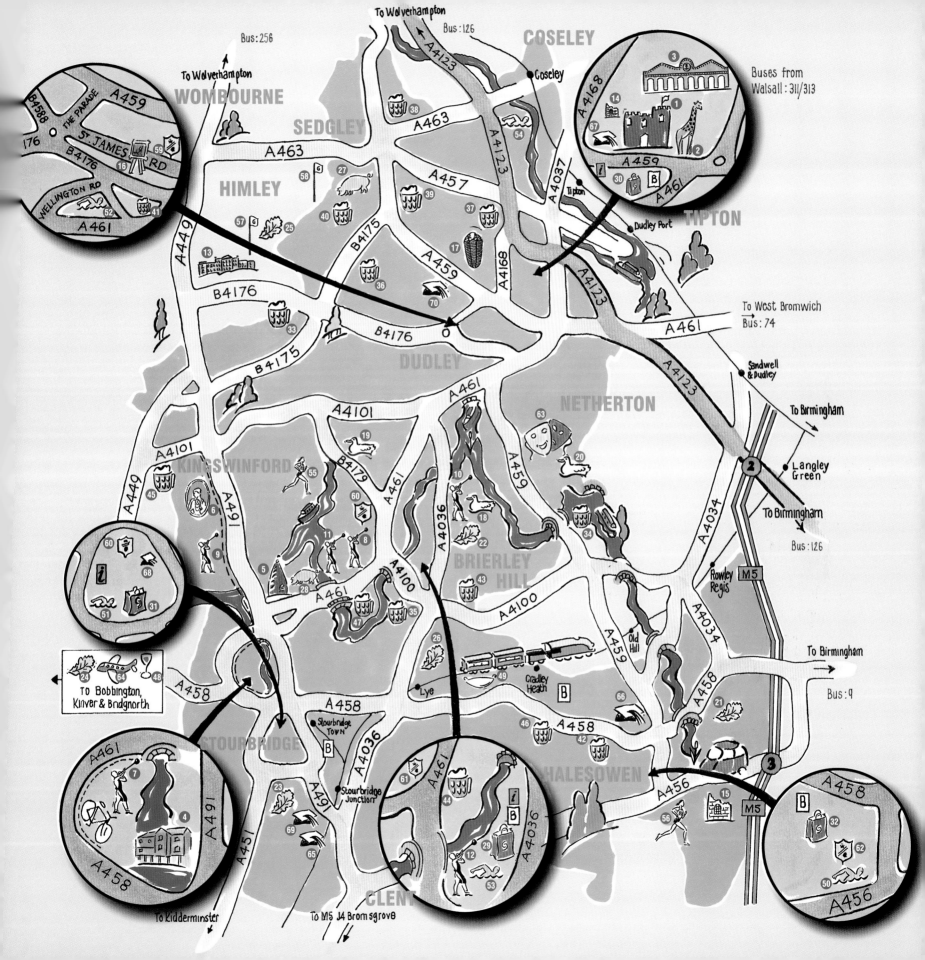

Dudley Town

Dudley was the centre of the West Midlands for nearly 500 years. In the Medieval period the Barons of the Castle were lords of an area from Kinver to Water Orton and from Belbroughton to Wolverhampton (including Birmingham). From the battlements of Dudley Castle they ruled all they surveyed.

Dudley town was their invention in the 12th century but its earlier origin in the open fields of the Anglo-Saxon period can still be observed in the curved narrow alleyways that run from the High Street. There has been a market in Dudley for over eight hundred years and whereas many street markets have long since gone, these latter-day burgesses still sell their wares from temporary booths within the market place.

The Medieval streets still survive and here in Dudley the original burgess plots can be made out in many of the narrow shop fronts that line the High Street. The two churches, locally known as 'top' and 'bottom' church, were here in 1180 and an example of a reliquery chapel still sits beneath the stone and iron 'top' church.

Over the period of time that Dudley has existed many styles of architecture have evolved and examples of structures from the last three hundred years abound; Finches's House in Wolverhampton Street built in the reign of Queen Anne, with its tablet dated 1707 and the 18th century buildings that line Stone Street Square including the Saracens Head pub.

Often the townsmen have attempted to emulate their great Medieval past and the Baylies Charity School (now the College) was constructed in stone in 1732. This was followed by Priory Hall in 1834, a good example of the Gothic revival. Modern architecture can also be found in the town. In the 1930s the Earl presented the Castle and grounds to the town to be made into a zoo. He employed Bertold Lubetkin to design ultra modern concrete structures, which even today look novel.

Dudley has its street furniture, typically grand as the centre of the Barony. The drinking fountain in Market Street, opened by Georgina, Countess of Dudley in 1867 together with its counterpart, the statue of her late husband Lord Dudley, erected in 1888 in the lower part of the town.

Dudley, unlike many towns was allowed to evolve slowly in the passing of the years. For this reason it is still a town to be seen and admired.

Dudley Market Place looking north-east down Castle Street, towards Castle Hill and St. Edmunds or 'bottom Church' as it is known locally.

The vista from the Castle battlements, looking west over the town that grew up to serve it.

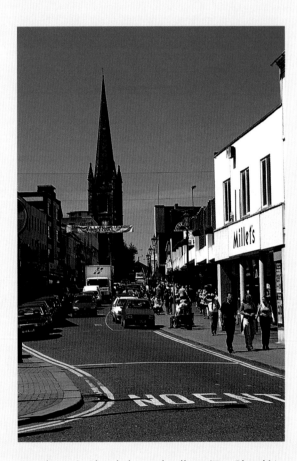

*St. Thomas's Church, known locally as 'Top Church' is a prominent
local landmark and is visible from a considerable distance.*

Since Medieval times, Dudley has thrived as a country market town. The daily open-air market and the adjacent enclosed Churchill shopping centre are both hives of activity.

19

Clockwise from top left:
Bainbridge Copnall's
Family Group, 1969;
The Apollo Fountain,
William Bloye, 1939;
Objects of Technology,
designed by Steve Field
and sculptured by John
Vaughan, 1994;
The Earl of Dudley,
Charles Bell Birch, 1888.

In flamboyant Italian Renaissance style, the 28ft high market place Drinking Fountain by James Forsyth, 1867. Made from local stone, this exquisite work was a gift to the town by the Earl of Dudley.

Dudley Castle

Dudley Castle is a place of contrasts. Once it was a place of activity amid the gentle countryside of Worcestershire, now it is a haven of peace amid the hustle and industry of the 'Black Country'. Once it stood as a proud fortification extolling the power of the Lords of Dudley, now it is a romantic ruin, a temple to the deprivations of time and weather.

First built around 1071, the history of the site is divided up into five main phases. The first Castle was constructed by the French Lord Ansculf of Picquigny and like many built at that time the walls and houses were of wood. The next family to occupy the site built again, this time in stone. Ralf De Paganal's Castle faced the first real test when it rebuffed a siege by King Stephen and gave Ralf cause to be thankful for the solidity of Dudley limestone, from which every subsequent Castle has been built. Alas Ralf's son, Gervaise, was not as astute as his father. He misread the political scene and ended up having to demolish the Castle as a punishment for rebellion. For a century there was no fortress on Castle Hill probably just a manor house, but in the 1280s a new family, the De Somerys began to rebuild.

Tradition has it that it was John De Somery, the bad baron of Dudley Castle, who completed the Great Tower and the new gateway. He is reputed to have robbed, pillaged and murdered to get the money for the building programme. He died in 1321 and as he was the last of the male line the Castle was passed to the Sutton family through John's sister.

England was, by now, a more peaceful place and the later Suttons contended themselves with the building of palatial new domestic wings within the Castle. Surviving from this period is the Castle chapel which once had a fine stained glass window and beautiful carved door. Much of the work was eclipsed however in the reign of King Henry VIII when its most powerful Lord, John Dudley, came to live in the Castle. From a position of disgrace John worked his way up to be to be Earl Marshall of England and Lord President of the King's Privy Council. John Dudley built over much of the work of his predecessors creating a fine renaissance palace, he climbed high and when he fell it was spectacular. His final act was to be beheaded on Tower Hill. Castles too were by this time in decline.

Many castles through the length and breadth of England were held by old families who sided with the King during the Civil war. In 1646 parliamentary forces attacked and took the Castle and the following year demolished its defences. Only the house remained and the family had long since moved out to their new house at Himley Hall. Shorn of its walls, gates and towers and bereft of its family, the Castle slumbered on for a further century before a fire in 1750 rendered it totally uninhabitable, a place of contrasts once more. Where once there were halls and chambers now only gaunt ruined walls remain. Where once the greatest in the land had disported themselves is now a home for rabbits and crows. Where once great men and women had laughed and cried now only the echoes of that great past endure.

Above: Dudley Castle, first built around 1071, stands as a sentinel overlooking the town, a reminder of its former glory and key position in English History.
Left: Looking up through the lofty remains of the Great Tower. Once a mighty fortress now partly shorn of it walls.

Built and improved over the course of many years, Dudley Castle reflects the passing ages through its variety of architectural styles.

Medieval days at the Castle and life in a bygone age are re-enacted by The Guild of the Blessed St. Edmund King and Martyr. Demonstrations feature weapons, armor, cooking, dress and music.

Shadows and silhouettes of the Castle's past.

The Tudor domestic range of buildings at Dudley Castle were built for John Dudley by his architect, Sir William Sharrington. It was a fine palace for a man who, during the reign of King Edward the sixth, became the most powerful Lord in England.

Maggie Howarth's exquisite cobblestone mosaics adjacent to the St. James's Priory recall the life of its inhabitants.

28

The now ruined Cluniac Priory at the southern end of Priory Park was founded around 1160 as a dependency of Much Wenlock, but eventually abandoned after the dissolution of the monasteries in 1580.

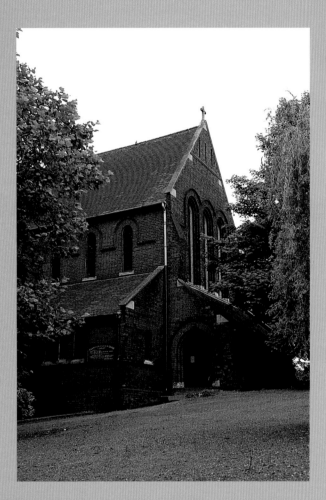

Left: *St. Chad's Parish Church, Coseley.*
Right: *Adjacent to the Church on Oak Street, The Old Mill, probably the most unusual dwelling place in the Borough.*

Housing estates in and around Dudley. **Bottom Right:** *The three once familiar tower blocks on Eve Hill estate. (Two of which have been demolished since the book went to print in July 1999).*

Wren's Nest National Nature Reserve, a unique fossil deposit dating back over 400 million years. Once, an ancient sea bed rich in marine life, then through powerful earth action, pushed upwards to form an almost vertical cliff face, the geological features of the reserve are fascinating in every respect. It is here where the 'Dudley Bug' as it is known was found in numbers by quarrymen who were excavating the area for limestone.

*The Courthouse,
Sedgley, standing at
the foot of All Saint's
Church. As its name
implies, it once dealt
out justice, it is now a
popular local pub and
deals out refreshment
instead.*

Sedgley

Sedgley was here at the first Millennium. Recorded in the Domesday Book, having fields, ploughs, woods, a priest, and people of varying status, feeding oxen and guiding ploughs. They built their homes, tilled their land, hewed their wood, were served by the priest and in turn served the Lord of the Manor.

At the heart of their community was the Bull Ring, the name given later, marking the cruel times of enraging bulls tethered amongst dogs bred to kill.

The Red Lion, a coaching inn, served passing travellers of bygone years. Older, the Court House, once dispensed manor justice for minor felonies, settled disputes and approved inheritances.

Through the years cottages and houses have slowly changed to shops, spreading up High Street, Dudley Street and easterly along Bilston Street.

Near the heart is the church, once 'mother' to nine villages whose paths all led there, trodden by tearful mourners, proud new parents and nervous brides and grooms. The paths can still be traced, bound for All Saints. Eastwards the Beacon tower marks the place where ancient signal fires once scorched its summit, sending news afar. Now modern telecommunications masts dwarf their predecessor. Changing seasons and a landscape constantly redrawn, still bring folk to its ridge to gaze at the splendid contrasts between east and west. Some gather early to celebrate dawn on Easter morn, others to 'dance in' May Day.

Gone are the scars of the nineteenth century industry, the overlying smoke of dozens of nails' hearths and their employment of children, the many broken limbs of workers in quarry, mine, furnace, forge and mill.

Times change, and one moment succeeds another. To the Bull Ring came the trams, first horse drawn, then steam powered, lastly electric. The crowds gathered to see them and the trolley buses that followed, before the motor bus ruled; and the shops, alongside, changed with them to meet each age.

Outlying fields sprouted new dormitory houses for workers preferring now to live away from work. The 'town' made room for supermarkets, and the consequences of the car.

Yet still, full of surprises, each street or lane can hold a hint of history, farms caught up within new housing, sudden glimpses of quiet sunny corners, with a place to sit, and through the partings, the panorama of the country.

At its heart still, the bustling shopping crowds, voices raised in greetings, above the passing traffic, will welcome the new Millennium.

Left: Sedgley Beacon, constructed in the early 19th century of Gornal stone, this three stage building was one of a string of message beacons which were spaced out along the length of the country to warn of impending attacks.

Above: The first day of May each year traditionally sees the First Sedgley Morris Men 'dance in' the dawn at Sedgley Beacon Hill.

A highly visible and cherished landmark, the spire of All Saints Church in Sedgley can be seen from a great distance. This structure was completed in 1829 and interestingly at one point during reconstruction, the original tower was encased within the existing one.

In Gothic style by the architect Thomas Lee, the All Saints Parish Church boasts superb examples of stained glass windows. These two panels, situated in the church alongside each other, give an interesting contrast between the different styles of glass work over the ages.

Dudley Street Sedgley, looking down towards the Clifton and the town centre.

Familiar landmarks in their own way; a local Georgian post-box built into a wall and the black and white half-timbered façade of the Mount Pleasant Pub.

Probably one of the best known pubs in the area (and probably the highest), The Beacon Hotel, is famous for its home brewed 'Sarah Hughes Ruby Mild', a potent dark beer brewed in the restored tower brewery behind the pub from an original recipe prepared by the present owner's grandmother.

Farmlands give way to urbanisation. Houses on the very edge of the Borough look across into Staffordshire.

The Gornals

The Gornals, Upper and Lower (Over and Nether) are two communities enjoying prevailing winds from across rural counties.

Upper Gornal sits on each side of the Turnpike Road running along the ridge. The older hamlet of Ruiton is here, where the finest views are enjoyed and houses and walls were once built from local stone. Gornal stone has long been used in gracious houses, humble cottages, churches and the solid field walls. Ruiton's Windmill stump, stands testimony to its strength and endurance.

In times gone, the people, reversing nature, ground the rock back to sand, by a horses power. The animal walked its circle, turned its wheel, until stone was dust again. *"Buy my lily white sond! A penny a bucket and a bit in yer ond."* Later industry took it, by the lorry load, for furnace lining. Gornal folk would travel the Midlands on caravan carts, some with sand, some with salt to savour, some to preserve food for winter.

The ridge, originally a lane for sheep became the main road, with church, chapels and pubs, school and shops.

Lower Gornal begins half way down the western slopes. The heart of its village is at Five Ways, where as the name implies, five roads meet. The numerous chapels show the old strength of Non-Conformity here; though Anglicans and Catholics are nearby too.

Anciently, trees remained to the west until the wood dwellers created their own clearing, in Gornal Wood; The Woodman Inn still provides the double meaning of place and trade. In Sedgley Church a plaque marks the times of John Bradley, of The Wood. Yet fossil trees employed its men, first at older shallow pits, then at nearby Baggeridge, a deep mine where horses joined men underground. The pit is now just a memory but the Miner's Welfare Club remains.

Years ago, Gornal women used their muscle to make bricks, mauling great lumps of clay, meeting their quota. Amalgamations and mechanisation changed all that. The many farms have gone too, and Ellowes is a school and not an ironmaster's mansion.

Yet with the inevitability of time passing so comes change, new housing, new shops, new library, new bank (Gornal thrift is legendary!), and these have made 'The Wood' the centre.

Hard times have brought people together. In village scale, and village warmth of character remains. To be shared with new generations, who make The Gornals their home.

Constructed from Gornal stone in the late eighteenth century, Ruiton Windmill stands, at one of the highest points in the area, as a testimony to the strength of this local building material. Its grinding wheels now long silent, it is still used, but now as a youth recreation centre.

A truly unique pub in the heart of Gornal Wood. The 'Crooked House' as it is aptly called, was victim to coal mining subsidence in the area. It can rightfully claim to be the only pub in the Borough where customers are staggering even before they have had a drink!

Above: *A blaze of colours as mothers are remembered on mothering Sunday, Gornal Wood Cemetery.*
Right: *A little further up the hill, some of the exquisite monuments that date back a few hundred years, stand silent in the tranquil church yard.*

*Local vistas in and around the
Gornals and London Fields area.*

Looking almost due west towards the village of Himley and Himley Park in Staffordshire. The edge of the conurbation.

Brierley Hill

A walk around Brierley Hill will reveal a modern looking mix of residential, commercial and shopping properties including some spectacular improvements engineered over the past 40 years.

The town developed on the briar covered slopes of Pensnett Chase because of the easily accessible coal, iron ore and fireclay. By 1765 its growing population justified the establishment of St. Michael's Chapel as an outpost of the ancient mother church of St. Mary's in Kingswinford, four miles to the north west. In 1848 it was created a separate parish confirming the area's recognition as a township. It continued to grow and became an Urban District within Staffordshire in 1894, expanding in 1934 by amalgamating with two adjoining local authorities, the resulting district covering what had been, more or less, the ancient Parish of Kingswinford. By a further local government reorganisation in 1966, the town became part of the Borough of Dudley.

Few people exploring the town today would know that it was once described as 'Hell on Earth', the place where the Devil died in despair on seeing an establishment to rival his own. The area was 'black by day and red by night' and a descriptive verse of the early 19th century was: *"When Satan stood on Brierley Hill, and far around him gazed, he said, 'I never shall again, at Hell's flames be amazed'."* It must have been quite a sight.

Today the opposite is true. Brierley Hill and indeed the rest of the Borough are places of clean air and open green belts with tight controls on pollution. The mining, steel and fireclay industries have long since abandoned Brierley Hill and they have been replaced by forward looking schemes set to last well into the next millennium. On the 300 acre site of the town's largest steelworks has risen one of the largest shopping and commercial complexes in Europe, the magnificent quality of the construction setting high standards for the country. Where once 500 pigs were slaughtered each morning before breakfast is a small square of shops which enhances what was already a fine High Street. An interesting estate of multi-storey apartments, an impressive sight form several angles and an outstanding local landmark, covers the mining honey-combed eastern slope of the town that runs alongside the Delph locks.

As the minerals became exhausted, properly planned housing estates, commercial developments and green parks covered over the scars of the area's industrial heritage. What was once an almost indescribable scene of fires and smoke now stands transformed, energetic and vibrant ready to face the challenges that lie ahead.

St. Michael's Church clock. I am told that it was once struck by lightening. Perhaps the more recently fitted lightning conductor and the missing numeral 'I' give proof to this shocking event.

Probably one of the most photographed vistas in Brierley Hill – the Delph Top Lock looking south on a hazy summers day.

*Numerous little work-
shops and factories
occupy the many,
somewhat aged, build-
ings along the canals
in the Borough.
Ingenuity, perseverance
and innovation prevail.*

Above: The Brierley Hill Police
Headquarters, fronted by a riot of spring-
time blossoms.
Right: The High Street and route down to
Amblecote and Stourbridge.

Sunset, as seen through winter trees in the churchyard of St. Michael's Church, Brierley Hill. (Just beyond the trees, out of sight, lies the large Royal Brierley glass factory).

Brierley Hill Market, High Street. With anything and everything on sale, the market is always a busy place and worthy of a visit.

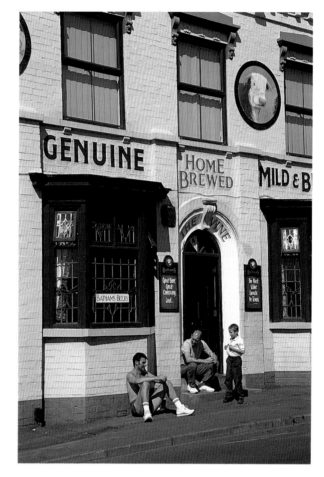

Right: The Vine, Delph Road. Some say that this is 'the' Black Country pub. A busy, down-to-earth sort of place with the best-known Shakespeare quotation in the BlackCountry across its frontage - 'Blessing of your heart; you brew good ale' - it is the home of Batham's beers and better known as The Bull and Bladder.
Far Right: Troutbeck and Withymoor Village form a panorama of houses when seen from the adjacent Stourbridge to Brierley Hill railway embankment.

A small part of the Merry Hill shopping complex. Spread over 125 acres with 1.5 million square feet of gross lettable area, 220 stores, 28 catering outlets and attracting over 20 million visitors per year, it is one of the largest in Europe.

Top: The lofted glass roofs of Merry Hill, advanced in architectural style, are a small part of a major shopping and recreation centre that attracts millions of visitors each year.
Bottom: Alongside the Waterfront commercial development, Merry Hill has become a vibrant and valuable amenity and resource to the Dudley Borough.

The Waterfront, a daytime business centre with its many
high tech office blocks, is transformed at dusk into the
Borough's most visited night life centre with its numerous
restaurants, nightclubs and pubs.

The Copthorne Hotel, the Borough's most prestigious hotel, overlooks the busy Waterfront area.

Bank's Brewers Wharf, a magnet for night life, sits at the busy entrance to the Waterfront basin.

A panorama of springtime flowers at the top edge of Quarry Bank's Stevens Park. The park, a gift to the town by Ernest Stevens, is a green and pleasant sanctuary alongside busy access roads.

Spring brings a colourful display to Quarry Bank.
Left: *The new walkway running parallel with the recently widened A4056.*
Right: *Blossoms veil Quarry Bank Church which has long stood as a cherished place of worship.*

Netherton

Netherton (Lower-town) unfolds southwards from Dudley Town to reach the Borough boundary with Sandwell, marked in the east and the south by the meandering Mousesweet Brook, which from its source in the Rowley Hills, *'chatters over stony ways'* to join the brimming River Stour at Cradley Heath.

Netherton itself is bisected by a waterway – The Dudley Canal – linking the Dudley Tunnel in the west with its Netherton counterpart in the east. The canal has been an integral part of Netherton's past. On its banks near Primrose Hill, anchors and chains for the maritime navies of the world were manufactured and tested, including those for the ill-fated Titanic! Today, those same banks carry walkers on the Netherton Trail or visitors to a Canal Boat Rally at 'Bumble Hole'. South of the canal lies Dudley Wood while to the west can be found Saltwells Wood, now part of the Saltwells Nature Reserve, a reminder of times past and an example of nature reclaiming a heritage once stolen by man and his industry.

The town centre of Netherton lies on both sides of the old Turnpike Road from Dudley to Halesowen. Now a modern metallic thoroughfare, this busy road whisks people past the change of catching a show at The Arts Centre or satisfying a thirst at Ma Pardoe's Pub, from where they could glimpse the statue of Joseph Darby (Josey the Jumper), one of Netherton's more famous sons, or study the now redundant Church School building, the site of which has housed a school since 1836.

Off the small market place can be found the entrance to Netherton Park, which stretches to Baptist End, where, it is claimed, total immersion of converts to the faith once took place, in a canal basin warmed by water from a local furnace! Also from the market place, Northfield Road runs down to Darby End where the nail makers from Derbyshire settled in the Black Country long ago.

Opposite The Old Swan pub (Ma Pardoe's), Church Road climbs to the highest point in Netherton, the site of St. Andrews's Church, plainly visible from all points of the compass for miles around. (With three Anglican and ten Non Conformist Churches, Netherton is not short of places in which to worship). From St. Andrew's the panoramic view takes in the hills of Worcestershire and of Shropshire as well as the more adjacent Black Country and the Netherton Reservoir, the 'top up tank' for the canal system, now a thriving centre for water sports.

Above: The statue and commemorative obelisk to the memory of the famed son of Netherton, Joseph Darby or 'Josey the Jumper', has since 1991 been a popular local landmark.
Right: Netherton Hill turns into a riot of colour in spring when the gorse blossoms and on a sunny day the display can be seen for miles. St. Andrew's Church dips over the horizon.

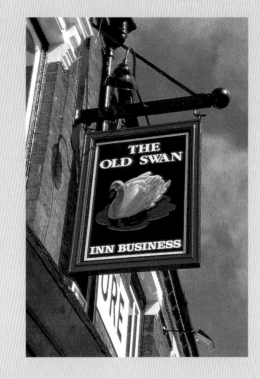

Top left: *An avalanche of household goods stream onto the pavement advertising the wares of the local DIY shop. The signage of its predecessors still advertises a long disconnected phone number.*

Top right and bottom left: *The Old Swan, or Ma Pardoe's as it is more affectionately known, was once one of only four home-brew pubs surviving in Britain. With is carefully preserved bar, it is still a much celebrated site for real ale and traditional pub enthusiasts.*

Bottom right: *Down Halesowen road lies the famed 'Allan's', a cornucopia for local shoppers. 'Supplying anything and every-thing' it is a shop where 'Yo cor ask for the wrong thing!'*

Looking south from St. Andrew's Churchyard a wonderful view unfolds; Lodge Farm Reservoir, Mushroom Green, Quarry Bank, Cradley and beyond to Clent Hills in the distance.

Windmill End with its classic black and white cast iron bridges and the distinctive Cobb's Engine House in the background.

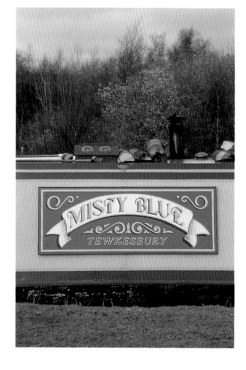

Clockwise from top left:
The Dry Dock in Netherton is a superbly redecorated old canalside pub. Complete with a narrow boat in the bar and is engine in the lounge, this is the home of the Desperate Dan 'Cow Pie'; Cyclists and walkers take on the challenge of the Netherton Tunnel, 2,768 meters long; Canals are an attraction for all ages; Passing canal boats find Windmill End a welcome stop.

The largest urban nature reserve in the country, Saltwells covers an area of nearly 100 hectares. It is a green oasis which boasts over 500 species of Moths and 32 species of Butterflies.

Mute Swans nest in a backwater in the Blackbrook Valley, part of the Saltwells Nature Reserve.

Kingswinford

Tradition asserts that Kingswinford, which is mentioned in the Domsday Book, derived its name from Sweyn, King of Denmark, the first of the Danish Monarchs who sat upon the English throne. Sweyn occupied the camp on Kinver Edge from 1002 to 1014 when 'Sweyn's Ford' came into use. Some ancient documents simply refer to it as Swinford Regis.

Kingswinford cross, on the old Roman road, has long been noted as a busy intersection. Driving in from Summerhill or Kidderminster, one is immediately faced with the welcome sight of the Cross Hotel which was first built in the early 17th century and then refronted a hundred years later. Directly opposite, and very definitely from a different century, the rather uniquely shaped electricity showroom takes corner position in the busy Townsend Place Market.

The early 19th century building in Compton Drive, heavily decorated with fine stuccoed moulded cornice and Ionic columns, is now, as the Broadfield House Glass Museum, home to one of the finest collections of English glass in the country. (It is also, so I have been told, home to the only fruit-bearing Mulberry tree in the Borough).

Kingswinford, not that many people know, also has a rather sinister claim to fame ... Out along the Wolverhampton road, just before the border with Staffordshire and dating back to the 1600's, stands Holbeache House. It was here, at the home of Stephen Littleton where the Gunpowder Plot conspirators found their last refuge. Whilst the group was being arrested, their leader, Robert Catesby was killed.

Alongside its history is a clear and positive indication of the areas intention to stake its claim in the future. The Pensnett Trading Estate, alongside other commercial and residential developments, has grown out of industrial wastelands and mine dumps to be one of the finest in the Borough.

The church yard at the St. Mary's Parish Church, Kingswinford, contains some of the oldest graves in the Borough. It has long been recorded in local history with parts of its architecture being of Norman construction. Its church cross, with gabled lantern-shaped head, dates back to Medieval times.

Top: *On the main Dudley Road, 'The Village' conservation area is a picturesque reminder of days gone by. The Old Court House built in the late 18th century, now a popular pub and hotel.*

Bottom: *The Village Pond and King George VI Park, alongside The Church of St. Mary.*

Top: The Cross Inn,
Kingswinford. Probably the
most well known landmark in
the area, stands proudly, as it
has since the late 18th century,
at the corner of Market and
High Street.
Centre: Kingswinford Cross is
a busy junction and the bench
opposite the Townsend Place
market is a good place to sit
and rest awhile.

The Cottage Inn High Street, well known for its hospitality and ornate frontage.

Children's playground, King George VI park, The Village.

Wordsley, the Hospital and King George V Park.

Above: Wordsley Hospital and Maternity Unit.
Right: High Street Wordsley. Cascades of spring-time flowers make this surely one of the best displays in the Borough.

Wordsley Parish Church, built to replace another that was threatened by coal mining subsidence in the area has, albeit with a brace around the steeple, stood the test of time.
Bottom left: *In memory of his 7 year old son, a terracotta tombstone made by Frederick Carder.*

*Evening shades reflect on the Stourbridge canal as it runs to the rear of the
Stuart Crystal Glass factory and the over 150 ft. high Red House glass Cone.*

Top: *The Rose and Crown and the late 18th Century Old Cat Inn, both on Wordsley High Street.*
Bottom: *Local architecture reflects the shape of the Red House Glass Cone; The Glass Factory Shop.*

Top: *The Fens Pool Nature Reserve, the largest area of open water in the Borough. It has recently been designated as a site of Special Scientific Interest because of the large numbers of amphibians that inhabit its waters.*
Bottom: *Trees on the Pensnett Trading Estate. Once a sprawling colliery, its gateway reflects its heritage.*

On Remembrance day each year, symbolised by the red Poppy which covered the fields of Flanders, those who gave their lives for the country are remembered.

Stourbridge

Stourbridge – Stuurbrug or Sturebrug as it is spelt in the 1255 Worcestershire assize roll – evidently owes its name to the ancient bridge erected across the River Stour which at one time formed the boundary of the counties Worcester and Stafford. It was a vibrant and prosperous market town which became important in the area for the production of woollen cloth.

The local coal, limestone and fireclay had been exploited on a small scale from early times but it was the 16th and 17th centuries that saw the birth of the Industrial Revolution, an event that would greatly change the fortunes of Stourbridge and its surrounding districts forever. The woollen trade declined and the ironwork, edge tools, nails, chains, bricks and heavy engineering took over. Canals and rail links were brought into town and this link to the major ports made it an important trading hub in its own right. Industrial Expansion encouraged population growth, improving living standards and social amenities. Glass manufacture was birthed in the area by 'gentlemen glass-makers' from France who had been forced to move their glassworks from woodlands to areas where there was coal with which to fire their furnaces.

In the 19th and 20th centuries the town saw dramatic change and development to its once heath-covered surrounds. The Town Hall that marked the Golden Jubilee of Queen Victoria was a marvel in its time and the Public Library built through the generosity of Andrew Carnegie changed the face of Stourbridge. In 1929 the district's greatest benefactor Ernest Stevens, presented the Studley Court Estate in Old Swinford, to the new Stourbridge Borough; it was to be known as Mary Stevens Park in memory of his beloved wife and the house on the land was converted into the Council House. Other benefactors over the years have included Thomas Foley who founded the Old Swinford Hospital School for poor boys. Virtually the whole of the parish of Pedmore was set aside to form part of the endowment of the school whose original building still stands. These great men and women have left their mark on countless generations. It was a golden age and Stourbridge was acknowledged to be one of the most progressive and pleasant towns in the Midlands.

Stourbridge and the adjacent areas of Pedmore, Amblecote, Old Swinford, Lye, Norton, Wollaston and Wollescote, each with its unique history, character and charm can boast as to their individual or collective achievements. Their new factories and developments, housing estates and schools are some of the best in the Borough. Intertwined with great achievements of the past, lies in today's generation, a spirit of determination that will ensure the success of the district's future in the years ahead.

Erected in 1857, the Stourbridge Town Clock has stood and watched the passing generations.

The silhouetted form of the Church of Our Lady and All Saints. Stourbridge Ring Road. (In case you are wondering, the top two red lines are a passing bus).

Continental delicatessen and café in Coventry Street.

Left: High Street. Banners fly in preparation for the annual Carnival Day, 1999.
Right: St. Thomas' Church, Market Street.

*Well connected by rail and road. **Clockwise from top left:** Stourbridge Town Station; Stourbridge Junction station clock (it is well worth waiting to hear this interesting time piece 'toot' and signal the passing of time); Station underpass & bus station.*

Top left: *Detail of artwork over the main entrance to the old Public Library, designed by Frederick Woodward and built with help from Andrew Carnegie the American philanthropist.*
Top and bottom right: *The fine buildings of the King Edward VI College in Lower High Street.*

Stourbridge Carnival Day. Crowds fill the town at this annual fun for all the family event.

Stourbridge Town, bounded by the ring road.

*A youngster enjoys the water jet at the Crystal Leisure Centre
swimming pools and indoor sporting facilities.*

Staring in apparent amazement and awe. A little painted lady.

Above; The Mary Steven's Park, a bequest to the former Borough of Stourbridge from Ernest Stevens, a local holloware manufacturer, in memory of his beloved wife, Mary. As it was intended, a place of enjoyment and relaxation for all. *Right;* The park's band stand is used throughout the summer for concerts of all types.

94

The entrance gates to the park and Queens Drive through its centre, the floral displays are always a welcome and colourful sight.

The foliage of exotic and indigenous trees transforms the park as the changing seasons paint their way through a palette of vivid colours.

Renowned for its outstanding academic achievements, the Old Swinford Hospital Boys School buildings are a prominent landmark. Established in the 17th century by the ironmaster Thomas Foley to provide education for poor boys, today the school attracts pupils from all over the United Kingdom and even other parts of the world.

Clockwise from top left: The annual Scout Movement parade that forms in Mary Stevens Park and marches up Heath Lane to St. Mary's Church; Dove Cote at one side of a graceful row houses at Old Swinford Cross; The recently restored Coach House under the shadow of St Mary's Church.

The powerfully contrasting, black and white timber-framed facade of the Old Swinford 'Castle'. With embattlements and turrets throughout, this building is an extravagant example of castellation.

The annual Stourbridge Navigation Trust's canal boat rally at the Bonded Warehouse in Stourbridge. A cavalcade of boats from all over the region.

The marvellously restored Bonded Warehouse which dates from 1799, was once where imported goods liable to excise duty were stored 'in bond' until claimed and paid for. It is only a short distance from here, where in 1829, the first steam locomotive to run in North America, appropriately named the Stourbridge Lion and the Agenoria for the Pensnett Railway were built.

*The viaduct at
Stambermill with its
ten brick arches,
completed in 1882 it
spans the River Stour.*

Lye, once famous for its nail, chain and brick making industries, has more recently become known for its colourful and aromatic string of almost adjacent Balti houses.

Above: *Lye, at the heart of what was once a highly industrialised area is still home to the internationally famous Folkes and Bronx Engineering Groups as well as the Helix Stationery Company.*

Left; *Allotments provide a touch of the country in the midst of busy urban areas.*

Right: *The green fields of Foxcote Farm overlook the town of Lye and the heart of the industrial midlands.*

*Almost directly on the Staffordshire/West Midlands border, The Forester's Arms
nestles in the Ridge wooded area, Wollaston.*

Freshly ploughed soil waits for springtime seeds on Racecourse Farm, Norton.

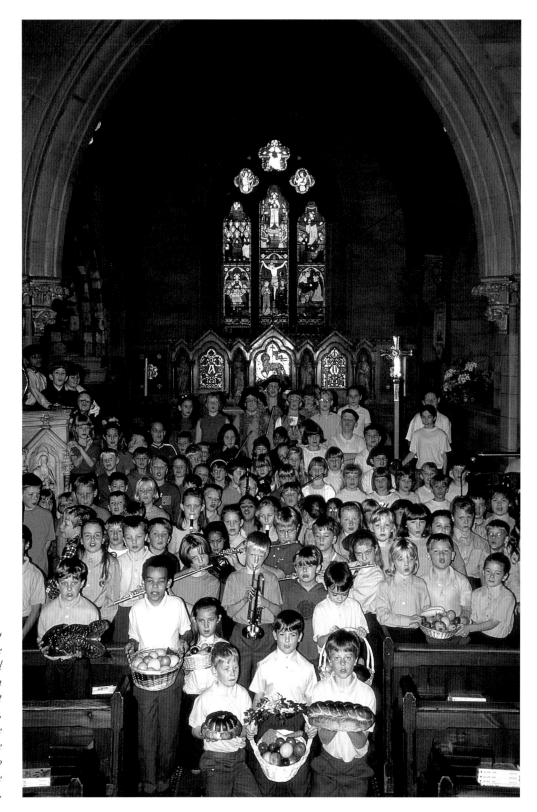

St Peter's Church, echoes to the sound of the Pedmore C.O.E. School Harvest Festival, an annual event for most schools in the Borough, an opportunity to give thanks to God for the harvest and to keep pupils in touch with the change of seasons.

Top: The pathway up to the Obelisk on Wychbury Hill, one of the Borough's most southerly points, gives walkers panoramic views over the area.

Bottom: Autumn fields, ready for harvest, overlook the Jacobean styled Wollescote Hall and the urban and industrial areas beyond.

Winter snows blanket sleeping farmlands (above) and summer storms bring refreshing rain in a contrast of seasonal change (right).

The slopes of Wychbury Hill, Pedmore, once the site of an ancient fortification, now rolling farmlands.

Halesowen

'We continued our walk to Halesowen, an ancient town squatting down among the hills on the little Stour'. A newcomer approaching Halesowen along the A458 at the top of Mucklow Hill would still recognize the location of the town as described in 1868 by The American consul in Birmingham, Elihu Burritt.

Halesowen was founded by Anglo-Saxon colonisers who built a small settlement in the sheltered valley of a stream, the Lacon, a tributary of the Stour. The town is first recorded in the Domesday Book of 1086 when it is referred to as Halas, a corruption of hwl – a topographical description of its location in hollows in the valley sides. The suffix 'Owne' was added in the thirteenth century and refers to the time when David ap Owen was Lord of the Manor. In 1214, on the order of King John a Premonstratensian Abbey was founded a short distance southeast of the town and under the influence of the Abbot, who became Lord of the Manor, the village flourished. In 1220 Halesowen a royal licence for a weekly market and annual fair was obtained and in 1270 Halesowen was first elevated to borough status.

Much later in the nineteenth century, Halesowen was known as the town of nailers. In backyard shops whole families slaved round the hearth from early in the morning 'till late at night. Today, no nailshops remain but in small factories the descendants of those nailors, several generations removed, still shape metal with the same diligence and application as their forefathers did before them.

With its tall slender spire, the magnificent sandstone church of St. John the Baptist, founded in 1083 is still the focal point of local loyalty and a symbol of continuity. The Medieval street pattern has been retained and some of the fine buildings, most of which are listed, preserved structures as diverse in character and age as the timber-framed Whitefriars, the Georgian buildings in Great Cornbow and the late-Victorian Methodist Church in Birmingham Street.

Halesonians are fortunate, for a few minutes walk from the town centre brings the rambler into ancient countryside criss-crossed by public footpaths in the byways of Lapal, Illey and Lutley. There too are the Leasowes laid out by the poet Shenstone and even a golf course with spectacular vistas over the town. Halesowen is a town 'in the country' on the edge of the urban sprawl.

Left & right: The slender spire of the Parish Church of St. John the Baptist, Halesowen. A landmark prominent in almost every Halesowen vista.

Sunset over Halesowen Town. The ever present spire of the church of St. John the Baptist.

A westerly view of Halesowen from the Haywood Embankment of the Dudley No. 2 Canal that runs alongside Leasowes park.

Manor Farm, Lapal. The green, most south-easterly fringes of the Dudley Borough. On a clear day the Wrekin, near Telford can be seen 47km (29 miles) away.

A powerful contrast between the old half-timbered cottages in Church Lane and the modern alluminium and glass Cornbow Shopping Centre, just a stone's throw apart in the centre of Halesowen.

As a haven for canal boats, the Hawne, or Halesowen Basin as it is sometimes called, marks the end of the navigable length of the Dudley No. 2 Canal.

Once one of the largest
tube mills in Europe
and now in early stages
of redevelopment, the
Coombeswood works lie
silent, a shadow of their
former glory.

The view of Uffmore Farm and the distant Clent Hills from Hayley Green.

Above: Fields of yellow Rape Seed contrast with the green trees of Halesowen.

Right: Founded in 1215, the now ruined St Mary's Abbey of the Premonstratensian Order at Illey played a major part in shaping the history of Halesowen.

The Leasowes,
A poet's landscape

The Leasowes is listed Grade 1 on English Heritage's Register of Parks and Gardens of Special Historic Interest. Covering 58 hectares, including Halesowen Golf Club, it consists of steeply wooded hillsides, rolling grasslands, small lakes, and streams incising their way through two narrow valleys. The land has always been utilised and tamed but not subdued. It is a little piece of wilderness in an industrialised urban area. Jealously guarded by the local community, the Leasowes is a much used and loved place for informal recreation.

Between 1743 and 1762 William Shenstone created a unique garden, recognised as a landmark in English Garden Design. Working with the natural landforms Shenstone, poet, painter and landscape gardener transformed a small grazing farm. He introduced cascades and pools into the watercourses and built objects of interest such as an obelisk and ruined priory. Seats and ornaments (often dedicated to friends and including inscriptions) were carefully placed. By removing trees in some places, and planting them to enhance in others, views and features were seen to best advantage.

The special character of the Leasowes is the combination of the genius of Shenstone who sought to bring forth *"The spirit of the place"* and its sheer quality of light, water, landform and flora. Summarised in the introduction to A Description of the Leasowes published by Robert Dodsley, William Shenstone's friend and publisher, in 1765;

Far from violating its natural beauties, Mr Shenstone's only study was to give them full effect. And although the form in which things now appear be indeed the consequence of much thought and labour, yet the hand of art is no way visible either in the shape of ground, the disposition of trees (which are here so numerous and striking) or the romantic fall of his cascades".

The Leasowes Restoration, to re-create the ferme ornée landscape of Shenstone, started at the end of the twentieth century. Owned, managed and being restored by Dudley Metropolitan Borough Council, the £1.8 million project is funded by the Heritage Lottery Fund, DMBC and the ERDF. The intention is to re-create a landscape which will be as authentic and beautiful as, but also more robust than, the original, as it now has to withstand the pressures of being a popular public park. Generations have enjoyed it, and will continue to do so in the next millennium.

Left: From 1745 the poet William Shenstone laid out walks, cascades and ornamental features in the woods to the east of Halesowen. With restoration works ongoing, the Leasowes (pronounced 'Lezzoes') will once again reflect much of their former beauty.
Above: Once epitomizing Shenstone's philosophy of picturesque gardening and intended as a gloomy, melancholic place, Virgil's Grove is still referred to by locals as 'the dark half-hour'.

As well as being classed as Grade 1 on the English Heritage Register of Parks and Gardens of Special Historic Interest, the Leasowes offers a range of recreational facilities for all the family, from a miniature railway to fishing and golf.

'Landskip should contain variety enough to form a picture upon canvas; and this is no bad test, as I think the landscape painter is the gardener's best designer. The eye requires a sort of balance here; but not so as to encroach upon probable nature. A wood, or hill, may balance a house or obelisk; for exactness would be displeasing…' William Shenstone, Unconnected Thoughts on Gardening.

125

Himley Hall

Himley Hall, the former home of the Earls of Dudley, stands in the rolling countryside west of Dudley. The house dates from the middle of the 18th century though it owes its present appearance to the modernising hand of the architect William Atkinson who remodelled it in the 1820's.

Himley had been one of the many manors scattered across 19 counties which William the Conqueror had granted to the Lords of Dudley. When their seat, Dudley Castle, was garrisoned for the royalists in the Civil Wars of the 1640's the family diplomatically removed themselves to the ancient moated manor house that then stood at Himley. As the profits from the coal and iron began to roll in from their estates in what was to become known as the 'Black Country' a larger house was needed to reflect their new wealth and status.

The new house needed a suitable park around it and in 1779 the fashionable landscape designer Lancelot 'Capability' Brown was called in. Half the village of Himley was swept away and the land incorporated into the enlarged park. Walks were laid out on the hill next to the house, carriage drives led to the lodges at the gates and rides were cut through the extensive woods. The most dramatic of the improvements was the creation of the Great Pool in front of the house, a feature which impressed many visitors at the time and many more since then.

The third Viscount was determined to enjoy his, by now, considerable fortune and filled the house with paintings and a notable organ for he was an avid enthusiast for Handel and his music. However he was willing to share his wealth with others. He supported soup kitchens in Dudley and the surrounding areas when the local industries went into one of their periodic declines and poverty became widespread. Happier events prompted oxroasts and other feasts when all and sundry were invited out to the park. In 1802, to mark the Peace of Amiens, he organised a great firework display setting a precedent for those organised by the Dudley Council today.

Visitors can enjoy the park and the woods and pools which now form part of the adjoining Baggeridge Country Park. The main ground floor rooms of the Hall have been renovated to accommodate a series of exhibitions which are open to visitors in the summer.

The annual Himley Park bonfire reflects across the darkness of the Great Pool.

Himley Hall, once the home of the Earls of Dudley, set in 180 acres of wood and parkland and built around 1740, was chosen for the honeymoon of the Duke and Duchess of Kent in 1934.

Dug out by hand in the 18th century, the Great Pool was a key element in 'Capability' Brown's scheme for the park; a fit setting for the house, and when seen from the house a focal point for his design.

The park sees a variety of activities including live shows, caravan rallies, and even hot air baloon launchings.

The grounds host the annual Dudley Show, Fireworks and Bonfire as well as being open to the public for fishing, golf, croquet and orienteering throughout the year.

Above: *The Rock Pool and Cascades, a series of pools which extend up the valley into the woods. Probably fish ponds in the Middle Ages but later incorporated into the 18th century landscaping.*
Right: *The views from the back wood look out towards Kingswinford.*

The Police Helicopter, a regular and indeed welcome sight around the Borough, lands on the rolling lawns in front of the imposing portico of the Hall's south face.

Night time family enjoyment comes to Himley Park once a year in the form of the winter bonfire and fire-work display. Held in November, the event remembers the infamous Gunpowder plot of 1605, the final gang members of which were rounded up just a short distance away at Holbeache House, Kingswinford.

In 1802 to mark the Peace of Amiens, the third Viscount held a great firework display which set a precedent for those organised by the Dudley Council today.

The Black Country Living Museum

In the shadow of Dudley Castle Hill, the Black Country Living Museum stands as a permanent reminder of the greatness of the Black Country.

It is also a testament to the foresight of the Dudley Council and many Black Country people who, starting in the 1960's, worked to preserve and portray something of the region's rich social and industrial history.

The museum began life on the Tipton Road site in 1975 and has transformed an area of derelict mine-shaft ridden land into one of the country's leading museums. Not one with dusty glass cases and 'do not touch' signs, but a centre for entertainment and enjoyment where people of all ages can see how 'the Black Country folk' lived and worked. It is simply, a step back in time, a life like and realistic regeneration of a fascinating age for all to enjoy.

Houses, shops, work places and civic buildings have been saved from throughout the region, carefully dismantled, moved and rebuilt, brick by brick. The centre of the Museum is the village area situated by the Dudley Canal and adjacent to the Dudley Tunnel. Here visitors can talk to costumed staff in the houses, shops, pub or chapel and watch skilled demonstrators at work in the chain shop, rolling mill, trap shop or boat dock.

Many visitors also choose to take a trip on one of the Dudley Canal Trust narrow boats into the spectacular limestone caverns hewn out of the very heart of the hills. Within the Museum they can also ride on an original electric tramcar, a horse drawn cart or one of the trolley buses made in nearby Wolverhampton. A lesson in the schoolroom reminds visitors of education in a different era, but even today's children enjoy the rides and stalls in the old time fairground.

The coal mining area includes examples of mining subsidence at the remarkable Tilted Cottage, a replica of the world's first steam engine, the Newcomen Engine originally built within a mile of the Museum and the Racecourse Colliery with steam winding engine, ventilation fan, tub trucks and pit frame. Visitors can don miners helmets and go, lamp in hand, 'Into the Thick' to experience the harsh working conditions of miners at the coal-face in the thick coal seams of the 1850's.

At the entrance to the site of the Museum, a major new visitor facility includes an introductory display about the Black Country and exhibitions which bring the story of Dudley, and the Black Country, into the present time. Here local manufacturers show how the skills and traditions which made Dudley famous are being further developed in the 21st Century to ensure the continuing prosperity of the town which is, the capital of the Black Country.

Shining copper kettles, reflecting images of a past age, hang in the window of the 'Canal Street Hardware Shop',
an Aladdin's cave of goods that were once an essential part of life.

The fires of the industrial revolution have long grown cold yet through careful care the past is brought back to life to demonstrate our forebears' ingenuity and skills. The plate from a boiler made just outside the Borough at Cradley Heath.

The images of a previous age are brought to life by costumed players amidst a reconstructed Black Country community.

*Black Country faces,
characters that form
part of, and bring to life,
the 'living' museum.*

The smell of individually baked fresh bread, the taste of fish and chips, and hand made sweets, all evoke memories of a past age.

Situated alongside the Dudley Canal, the museum adjoins the northern portal of the Dudley Tunnel which was hewn as an entrance to the underground limestone mines located beneath Dudley Castle.

Travelling through the long and dark disused tunnels into the very heart of Castle Hill, visitors can only marvel at the immensity of the achievement around them. Not only that of the original construction and opening in 1792, but that too of its partial reconstruction two hundred years later.

Canals in the Borough

Two centuries ago saw the birth of the industrial revolution.

Dudley was at the forefront of industrial development having both the natural resources of coal, limestone and clay and an abundance of local labour and skills to provide for the demands of the iron, glass and brick industries.

In order to provide local factories and mills with their much needed raw materials and to supply the cities and ports with finished goods, the Dudley and Stourbridge canals were built. These water-filled highways connected Dudley to the Birmingham Canal at Tipton and Tividale, the Worcester Birmingham Canal at Selly Oak and the Staffordshire and Worcester Canal at Stourton.

Access was made into the limestone mines at Dudley Castle and Wren's Nest as early as 1778, in order that this vital resource could be taken directly to the lime kilns and iron works in the area. With the development of the railways, interchange basins were constructed at Netherton, Stourbridge and Halesowen for the transfer of goods. The canals were a vital artery that fed and nourished the revolution that would in turn impact the world.

Today, with the advent of high speed trains and the motorway systems the canals are a much quiter place. The almost long-gone art of narrow boat building can still be seen at Dadford's Shed near the base of the Red House glass cone at Wordsley; through constant maintenance one can travel up the 200 year old flight of locks at the Delph in Brierley Hill or through the nearly two mile long Dudley Canal Tunnel. The canal towpaths no longer reverberate to the heavy thud of horses hooves yet the canal walkways are still a major route for walkers, hikers and cyclists. The once busy canals themselves now also act as a quiet haven for wildlife providing an area of peace and tranquility in this modern bustling world.

Note: As the canal system is an integral part of most towns in the Borough, it is portrayed on various other pages of this book, these images are but a taster.

The character and charm of the English Narrow Boat. Once a vital form of transport, now a unique way of exploring the past, a tranquil pastime or just a quiet break from it all.

Boats moored in the quiet basin adjacent to Dadford's Shed, named after Thomas Dadford, the engineer responsible for the design and building of the Stourbridge Canal.

Just up from Dadford's Shed on the Stourbridge Sixteen is a brick built roving bridge which spans the entrance to a quiet side pond and basin and is overlooked by the attractive general store knows as 'The Dock'.

The Delph Locks, an inspiring 19th Century canalscape which, through a series of eight (once nine) locks, raises or lowers the Dudley No. 1 Canal by eighty five feet.

The bright swirl of colours that adorn most Canal Ware is a unique and attractive art form in itself.

Dudley Zoo

In the grounds of the Dudley castle, one of the oldest and highest landmarks in the area, Dudley Zoo has long been home to some of the world's biggest, rarest and highly exotic animals.

When opened in May 1937, it was considered the most modern zoo in Europe, with its 50-acre wooded site it still proves a top tourist attraction – as thousands of photo albums testify.

Throughout the years the keeping of all animals at Dudley Zoo and their welfare has been of prime importance, a fact now reflected in the ongoing international breeding and conservation programs which hopefully, will protect many endangered species for future generations. Such animals include Asiatic lions, lemurs, penguins, chimps, orangutans, dwarf crocodiles, Madagascan pink pigeons, Walrapp Ibis and Arabian Oryx. While most of these animals are from distant lands, Dudley Zoo experts are also helping on the home front with native species, including red squirrels, crayfish and great crested newts.

There is an active underground movement too – beneath the Zoo site lies an extensive network of limestone caverns which now house a colony of endangered bats. The caverns are also occupied by the fossilized remains of trilobites (known locally as the Dudley Bug), a distant relative of which, the triops, or Tadpole Shrimp – one of the oldest living species in the world has been saved from extinction by Dudley Zoo's conservation crew.

And that's the way forward as Dudley Zoo enters the new century, the work carried out during the past sixty years will continue with an ongoing emphasis on education, conservation and enjoyment for all.

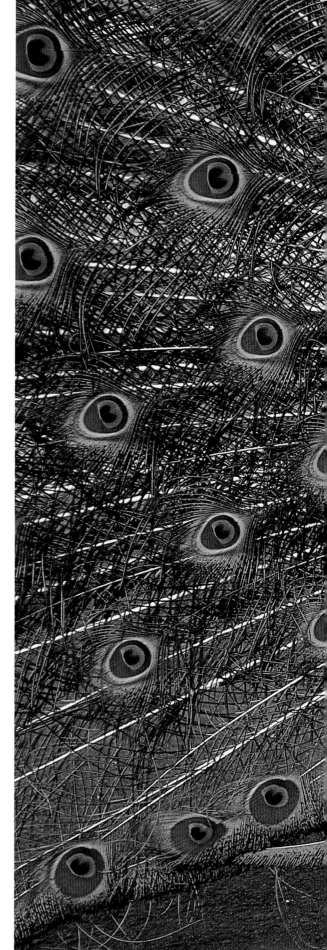

A bright flurry of dazzling Peacock feathers.

Top: *The Zoo's oldest inhabitants, one of a group of eight flamingoes that have been at the zoo for a remarkable 40 years.*
Right: *The Zoo boasts a large variety of creatures great and small from every continent.*

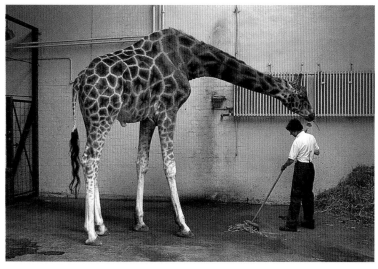

Duncan Edwards, Footballer,

1936-1958

"I considered him to be the finest young player in England at that time. Surely he would have gone on to be one of the greatest players the world had ever seen". Bobby Robson.

Duncan Edwards was born in Dudley on 1 October, 1936 and throughout his short life professed his pride at being an ambassador for the town wherever his football career took him. His name will forever be associated with Manchester United and the so-called 'Busby Babes', a concept developed by United's Manager Matt Busby in the late 1940's when the club was badly in debt and unable to afford to buy 'expensive' players. He first played for the club when he was only 16 years and 185 days old and just three and a half years later, Duncan celebrated his 100th appearance for United.

Tragically he was killed along with seven other members of the team when their aircraft crashed in Munich on the 21st of February, 1958. Five thousand people attended his funeral at Dudley Cemetery. There was not a dry eye among them.

As a tribute to this young man and as a celebration to his life a set of stained glass windows were installed in St. Francis church and a statue to his memory was set to be unveiled towards the end of 1999.

The two stained glass memorial windows, showing Duncan Edwards in both his Manchester United and England strip, can be seen in St. Francis' Church, Priory Estate. A display case, containing some of Duncan's shirts can also be found at the Dudley Leisure Centre.

James Butler, RA works on the modelling of the figure of Duncan Edwards, prior to detailed portraiture and casting (June, 1999). The final work is scheduled to be unveiled in Dudley town centre towards the end of the year.

Public Art

As the 'capital' of the Black Country, the Dudley Metropolitan Borough contains a wealth of truly exceptional pieces of Public Art from every century and in every material and technique. There are splendid bronzes - from the Art Deco style figure of Apollo outside the Council House, to the statue being cast as this book went to press, of the legendary Dudlean footballer, Duncan Edwards. There are magnificent concoctions of stone, such as James Forsyth's exuberant fountain of sea horses in the Market Place, a companion to the Perseus fountain at the Earl of Dudley's former home, Witley Court, or the stone 'Christ' embracing Mary Magdalene at Gornal Wood. There are even figures made of glass, such as the portraits by David Reekie of Cedric Hardwicke the film star, and Frederick Carder the glass designer who gaze down on us from the stairway of Stourbridge's Crystal Leisure Centre. A thousand tiny fragments of glass mosaic coalesce to form the images of birds in the pavings adjacent to the glassblower statue at Stourbridge Station, the glistening skin of the whale at Belle Vue Sculpture Trail, or the irides-cent wings of "Pegasus", Dudley's Millennium symbol by Andrew Logan.

There are inscriptions too - from the words of Thomas Hardy etched on Dudley's war memorial tower, to a passage from Robert Dodsley's eighteenth century guidebook to the Leasowes carved into a simple and timeless slate bench, put there as the tribute of a great twentieth century poet and artist, Ian Hamilton Finlay to a great poet and artist of the past, William Shenstone. We can find also the brave lines from the speeches of Thomas Attwood, the political reformer, inscribed on a representation of 'his' Great Reform Bill literally made concrete on the Stourbridge Road near his birthplace in Halesowen, and we can find the younger voices of today, poems by children from a Coseley School printed on to the glass windows of Coseley Station.

Everywhere a wealth of tiny detail awaits those who wish to find it : the golden arrow of St. Edmund wings its way across a railing at St. Edmunds Church; lead 'putti' capture the rainwater on the Edwardian façade of Dudley Library; the deli-cate tracery of a metal spiders web forms part of the gate of the new Brockmoor Primary school.

Dudley's artworks in public spaces speak not only about the past and present, but also of the future.

Andrew Logan applying mirrored mosaic to the wings of the small version of 'Pegasus', June 1999. The large version of which is to be a Millennium Commission for Dudley and is to be installed alongside the new southern by-pass.

Clockwise from top left: Memories of Dudley, Paula Woof, 1988; Coseley's children cast precious playthings to form metal pavers at the local railway station; Stainless steel cylinders reflect mosaic images of birds laid in the pavings adjacent to the glassblower statue at Stourbridge Station; A panel from the Stourbridge war memorial that honours the dead of two world wars.

The 'Industry' mural, by Steve Field, is part of a whole series of artwork in the smallest park in the Borough, Pocket Park, Lye. Opposite another mural which depicts the Lye Carnival and overlooked by a cast iron clock, this series of works celebrates the history and modern day life of the town.

A recently completed graffiti mural adds colour to a side wall behind the Mitre Inn, Stourbridge. A team of six artists going under the collective name of 'Artbeat' and using just aerosol spray paints, have transformed what was once a dark parking lot into a colourful modern day gallery. (June 1999).

The Glass Quarter

The Glass Blower statue, situated in Stourbridge at one end of the area known as the Glass Quarter, celebrates 400 years of glass making in the district.

"Glass is one of the true fruits of the art of fire".
Antonio Neri, The Art of Glass, 1612.

Glass has been made within the Borough of Dudley since the late 16th century when French Lorraine glass-makers settled in the area. Attracted by the rich deposits of high quality fireclay needed to make the pots that hold the molten glass, the immigrant glass families of Tyzak, Henzey and Henzell laid the foundations of a glass industry which after four hundred years remains the greatest glassmaking area in the country.

Known as Stourbridge glass because the shipping of products and banking were carried out mainly from that town, the main areas of glassmaking were based in Dudley, Wordsley, Amblecote and Brierley Hill.

In the 17th century, bottle and window glass were the staple products probably using local sands for the raw material while the local coal deposits provided the fuel for furnaces. During the 18th century the glass companies began to use the new English lead glass which had been invented by George Ravenscroft in London in the 1670's. Glass cones, brick conical structures housing the furnace with the glass pots surrounded by teams of glass-makers, became a feature of the landscape often built adjacent to canals to give easy access for raw materials and shipment of finished products.

In the 19th century the glass-makers developed their skills even further and created such a kaleidoscope of colours, shapes and decorative techniques that the period can justifiably be called the golden Age of Stourbridge glass. Processions of glass-makers at public holidays reinforced the feeling of community spirit amongst the workers.

Stourbridge not only influenced other countries with their glass products but also exported glassmakers such as John Hill who set up the Waterford factory in Ireland and Fredrick Carder who was responsible for establishing Steuben Glass in Corning, New York State, America's finest glass works.

The industry continues to be a fascinating mix of craftsmen, from the single glass-cutter working alone in his cutting shop, to a specialist company producing glass rods and tubing, to the large traditional cut glass factories and new glass studios operated by college trained graduates. Fresh initiatives by large and small companies in the areas of cameo, coloured, cut and engraved glass forecast exciting innovations based on four centuries of tradition.

The Broadfield House Glass Museum in Kingswinford, a past 'Best Small Museum' winner, celebrates the magical art of glassmaking and features the very best of British glass. The museum building itself combines the old with the new; a beautiful Georgian house with an award-winning modern extension, believed to be the world's largest all-glass structure.

Iridescent aquamarine vases, a tribute to past generations of glass-makers and collectors items of the future. Individually hand-made in the Borough by Okra Glass Studios, Brierley Hill, who like a number of other glass factories and studios continue the glass making tradition.

Left: *Molten glass is taken from the furnace at which point it has the consistency of treacle and is at approximately 1,100 degrees centigrade. Truly, 'fruits of the fire'.*

Bottom: *A number of local glass manufacturers and studios have created limited editions of works especially to celebrate the turn of the century. 'Firedance' by Sarah Cowan.*

Right: *Alongside the more traditional crystal glass new expressions of the glass-makers art. Clockwise from top left: Layered Glass bowls & coloured bottles, The Blow Zone, Stourbridge. Traditional glass cutting, Red House Glass Cone, Wordsley.*

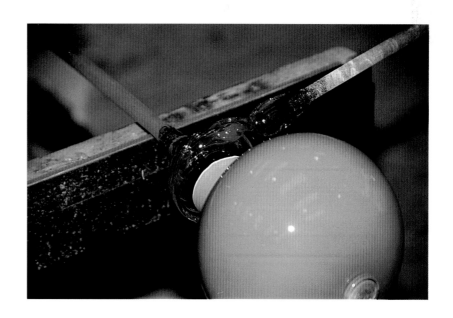

The Living Countryside

'Dudley is blessed with a rich and varied countryside - an important asset to the Borough and to its residents and visitors'.
Dudley M.B.C., Dudley Countryside Strategy, 1994

The countryside in Dudley is a largely man-made environment, but contains a wealth of ecological, geological and historic interest, as well as important landscapes and recreation facilities. Geology has an acknowledged importance in Dudley. It provided the raw materials that led to the development of the Black Country, has shaped topography and land drainage patterns, continues to influence plant and animal communities, and offers opportunities for scientific research. Many post-industrial sites are recognised for their nature conservation value. Wrens' Nest, exploited for centuries for its limestone, is recognised internationally for its fossils, being declared a National Nature Reserve in 1956. Skilled guides lead groups through the reserve giving them hands on experience of what is one of the most famous geological sites in Britain.

Saltwells Wood was largely planted by Lady Dudley in 1795 to hide the scars of coal-mining. It is now one of our finest Bluebell woods, also supporting many bird and insect species. The Fens Pools, previously excavated for clay, support several breeding and wintering birds and also have one of the largest populations of Great Crested Newt in the country.

Successive generations have each left their mark on the landscape, superimposing upon, but rarely obliterating, the features of previous land use. The earliest evidence of human occupation rests with 8,000 year old Stone Age flints discovered in fields in southern parts of the Borough. The strategic importance of the area is witnessed by the remains of Wychbury Hill Fort (built about 500 BC by an Iron Age clan), Roman roads (some built during the invasion period of the AD 60s) and Dudley Castle (founded shortly after the Norman Conquest).

More passive medieval manors, 18th century estates and the Victorian era have each influenced the area further. Much of the countryside has been traditionally farmed, albeit more intensively during modern times. However, many meadows, woods, hedges and ponds still remain, providing valuable refuge for wildlife and significant features in the landscape.

The countryside in Dudley provides plenty of opportunity for public enjoyment. A dense footpath network allows direct and easy access, offering the chance to escape the stresses of urban life, to gain exercise, to appreciate the local environment and to explore the countryside on our doorstep.

Left and above: *'The Bluebell is one of Britain's best-loved flowers, not particularly as an individual plant, but en masse. The sight and scent of a Bluebell wood in spring is one of the most striking in the British countryside; indeed, it is something of a British speciality'. The Old Oak in Bluebell Wood, Wychbury Hill.*

The countryside in the Dudley Borough, if you take the time to stop and look, is a riot of colours, a veritable living showcase of flora and fauna. An excellently produced set of guides covering many local walks, nature reserves, flowers, butterflies, fauna and a range of other subjects are available from all tourist offices and libraries. They have helped me to explore the many delightful countryside beauty spots within the Borough, I am sure they will you too.

A word of special thanks:

As a token of my thanks for her patience, longsuffering and understanding, I promised my wife, Vanessa, some flowers when I finished this book. She loves all of my pictures of flowers in the Borough, so here they are, 'a bunch of the best' …

Acknowledgements

I wish to extend my grateful thanks to the many Borough departments, organizations, companies and individuals who have advised or assisted me in my work on this project. The list is in no particular order and I extend my apologies to any that I may have unthinkingly omitted.

Abstract Media
Alan Peace
Alan Harris
Alec Connah
Black Country Living Museum
Black Country Society
Blow Zone Glass Studio
British Trust for Conservation Volunteers
Broadfield House Glass Museum
Buckpool & Fens Pools Nature Reserve
Bumble Hole Local Nature Reserve
Campaign for Real Ale
Caroline Redley
Charles Advertising
Chris Green
Christopher Gallagher
David Hill
Dudley Arboricultural Department
Dudley Art Council
Dudley Canal Trust
Dudley Castle & Zoo
Dudley Cave Rescue Team
Dudley Countryside Management

Dudley Libraries
Dudley Marketing Initiative
Dudley Metropolitan Borough Council
Dudley Planning & Leisure
Dudley, Stourbridge & Halesowen News
Dudley, Stourbridge & Halesowen Chronicle
Dudley Tourist Information Centre
Dudley & West Midlands Zoological Society
Emma Middleton
First Sedgley Morris Men
Friends of Dudley Castle
Friends of Dudley Zoo
Friends of The Leasowes
Garry Cooper
Geoff Holt
Hawbush Urban Farm
Himley Hall & Park
J.O.A. Advertising
Jeff Jephcott
Jill Hitchman
John Holme
Julia Lockett
Julie Haney

Katherine Finney
Leasowes Park
Lt. Harry Knock (Retired)
Merry Hill
Margaret Roberts
Mike Fox
Okra Glass Studio
Paul Watson
Portia Howe
Police Helicopter Services
Royal Brierley Crystal
Royal Doulton Crystal
Saltwells Local Nature Reserve
Stuart Crystal
Stuart Dodd
The Design Centre
The Royal British Legion (Stourbridge)
Tom Slater
Tracey Ruddle
Viv Astling
Vic Smallshire
Wren's Nest National Nature Reserve

Bibliography

A Black Country Photographer, Frank Power, 1996
A Brief Intimate Story of Netherton and St. Andrew's Church
     L.E. Homer
Black Country Living Museum, Pitkin, 1999
Buildings of Special Architectural or Historic Interest
     Dudley M.B, 1989 (Updated)
Canal City, Michael Pearson, 1998
Countryside Strategy, Dudley M.B., 1994
Dudley Canal Tunnel, Dudley Canal Trust, 1993
Duncan Edwards – Manchester United and England
     Geoff Warburton, Dulston Press
Himley Hall and Park: A brief History, David Radmore, 1996
Memories of Dudley, 1996, Alton Douglas, Beacon
     Broadcasting
Official Guide, Dudley M.B., 1996
Planning & Development Handbook, Dudley M.B., 1995

Public Art Guide, Dudley M.B., John Bennett, 1991
Public Art Review, Dudley M.B., 1994
Public Art Strategy, Dudley M.B., 1999
Stourbridge Information Guide, 1998
Stourbridge in Times Past, JackHaden, 1980
Stourbridge, Old and New, 1908
Stourbridge, Wollaston & Amblecote, Sutton, 1997
The Art of Glass, Antonio Neri, 1612
The Blackcountryman, various issues
The History of Netherton C. of E. School, 1986, Peter Crofts
     & Dennis Lewis
The Holy Bible, New International Version,
     International Bible Society, 1984
The Netherton Trail booklet, Hillcrest School, 1997
The Schoolmistress, William Shenstone
Walks in the Black Country and its Green Borderland,
     Elihu, Burritt, 1868
William Fowler's Kingswinford, Eric Richardson, 1999

Photo Credits

With sincere thanks to those who contributed images to help bridge the gaps in my collection. Thank you too for the many who sent in excellent pictures which, only because of limited space, were not included. Photos are all listed in order of appearance.

All photos © Rob Birkbeck, 1999 other than those listed below;

J. Arthur Beddard, pages 1 & 23
Vanessa Birkbeck, pages 5, 96, 97, 100a, &167b
Andy Newell, page 9
Dudley M.B.C. Information Section, page 10
Eric Matty, page 11
Steve Field, pages 20d 28, 154, 155a, 155b, 155c and 158
Danielle Birkbeck, pages 30a, 124b and 127
James Birkbeck, page 49a
D. J. Hubball, pages 93, 138, 139c, 140 & 150
Black Country Living Museum, pages 139a, 139b, 139d & 141

Nick Fazey, page 142a
Geoff Warburton, page 146b
Simon Bruntnell, page 153
Okra Glass Studios, pages 159 and 160
Paul Ras, page 161a, 161c & 161d
Brian Jones, page 164c
Jonathan Preston, page 164d

Cartography

Map on pages 14 & 15 © Dudley Marketing, 1999
    Created by J.O.A. Marketing & used with permission.

On Assignment

Thank you to my family, who faithfully carried my bags, tripod, cameras and other various items on many a photo shoot. We came home late, covered in mud yet the times spent together will never be forgotten. Exploring the Borough has given us all a deep love for the place in which we live.

A Time for
Everything

There is an appointed time for everything and there
is a time for every event under heaven —

A time to give birth and a time to die.
A time to plant and a time to uproot what is planted.
A time to kill and a time to heal.
A time to tear down and a time to build up.
A time to weep and a time to laugh.
A time to mourn and a time to dance.
A time to throw stones and a time to gather them again.
A time to embrace and a time to shun embracing.
A time to search and a time to give up as lost.
A time to keep and a time to throw away.
A time to tear apart and a time to sew together.
A time to be silent and a time to speak.
A time to love and a time to hate.
A time for war and a time for peace.

He has made everything appropriate in its time.

I know that there is nothing better for them than
to rejoice and to do good in one's lifetime.
Moreover that every man who eats and drinks sees
good in all his labor — it is the gift of God.

Ecclesiastes 3